AF571750

101 FUN HUGS

By Ed Fischer

101 action, laugh-out-loud hugs, plus warm, caring messages

To daring, caring people
everywhere, but especially to
Jackie, Pam, Becky, Paula,
Jessica, Lavonne, Jeff and
all the special people in
my life.

To order more books write or call:
Ed Fischer
57 Viking Village
Rochester, Minnesota 55901
Telephone 507 281-5119

OTHER ED FISCHER BOOKS:

* 'What's So Funny About Getting Old?'**
* 'God Grant Me the Laughter'**

(**CompCare publishers)

* '101 things to do with lutefisk'
* '101 uff das'
* 'Minnesota: A Cold Love Affair'
* 'The Caretoon health calendar,' 365 cartoons, quotes and tips.

Printed by Modern Printers, Faribault

ISBN 0-9624482-3-0

HOW TO USE THIS BOOK:

1. Read and laugh yourself silly.
   (Share with a friend)

2. Copy or clip a favorite hug and/or caring message and put it up on the refrigerator.

3. Pick a number at random and do one or more hugs.
   (Any number can play)

4. Be bold - do all the hugs with someone special.

How to approach someone to hug for the first time...

When to hug...

- When someone you care about is hurting.
- When you're hurting
- In the morning
- In the afternoon
- At night
- Saying goodbye
- Saying hello
- When it's cold
- After an argument
- After Someone fixes the toilet
- When you don't have the words to say I care for you and I need you
- When you just need to be touched!♡

'Love cures people. Both the ones who give it, and the ones who receive it.'

-Karl Menninger

101 HUGS

Whereas this book was made to be funny and a little silly, it's other purpose is to get you and the special people in your life to lighten up and hug with gusto.

-Ed Fischer

2. against the wall hug

3. burp like a baby hug

4. hug and give a back rub

'To love and be loved is to feel the sun from both sides'
-David Viscott

5. check fat on waist hug

6. hug and shake

7. hug and mess your partner's hair

'Laughter and tears are both responses to frustration and exhaustion. I myself prefer to laugh since there is less cleaning up to do afterwards'

-Kurt Vonnegut

8. hug and moan

9. write a letter on your partner's back with your finger – then have them guess the letter hug

10. hug and sway to music

"People need loving the most when they deserve it the least."

– John Harrigan

11. forgive someone for something (or forgive yourself) Say it and hug

12. wrap in rug hug

13. the `dip' hug

14. both wear fluffy sweaters
hug

15. more than two people
hug and shuffle.

"The heart that loves is
always young."

—Greek proverb

16. hug in shower with clothes on

17. Surprise hug (click partner's nose)

18. hug and tap dance hug

'A laugh is happiness set to music.'

-william Rotsler

19. hug a senior citizen
(or the oldest person there)

20. Bunny hop hug
(hum the music)

'Youth is a gift
of nature, but age
is a work of art.'
- Garson Kanin

21. share an intimate feeling hug

'The main thing in life is not to be afraid of being human.'

-pablo casais

22. hug and sing a song

23. hug in the same big shirt

24. hug on a sofa

25. Surprise-squirt water down Pants* with water pistol hug

*or shirt

'Everything is funny as long as it happens to somebody else'

-Will Rogers

26. appreciate the environment... hug a tree

27. little puppet behind the back hug

'Be cheerful - if nothing else, it'll drive people crazy'

—Anonymous

28 the little kid hug

'To love is a glimpse of heaven'
– Karen Sunda

29. Squeeze and let go - squeeze and let go - squeeze and let go - squeeze and let go . .

30. pet hug

'Anyone who has a dog to make him feel important should also have a cat to keep him humble'

31. hug and lift partner

32. hug, lift and twirl partner

33. hug in the rain

'Too much of a good thing can be wonderful.'
—Mae West

34. hug and tell a joke (sample jokes on next page)

'If you've heard this story before, don't stop me, because I want to hear it again.'
—Groucho Marx

35. hug and move butts in circular motion

Sample Jokes...

I went to a movie. The movie was so bad, everyone stood in line to get out.

I like sports. Today I played real bad. I even lost a ball.
Don't feel bad. Lots of people lose golf balls.
I was bowling.

Coffee can be bad for you. I know someone who went blind drinking coffee.
She kept leaving the spoon in the cup.

I went shopping. What a store! If you ask for something under $100 , they look in their garbage.

'One good laugh will relax your stomach muscles for 45 minutes.'
-Robert J. Wicks

36 Scratch my back -
I'll scratch yours hug

37. Sneak up
behind someone
hug

38. hug in stocking feet
(walk with partner on feet)

'Real love stories
never have endings'
-Richard Bach

41. hug and whisper sweet nothings

42. hug while holding partner's leg

(the Harpo Marx hug)

43. hug and bump

44. guess what I just ate hug

45. guess what's behind your back hug (10 guesses)

46. hug and rub noses

47. you have 5 chances to guess who I am hug

48. Royalty hug: kiss on both cheeks, then hug

49. the humble hug

'Learn to pause... or nothing worthwhile will catch up to you'

– Doug King

50. animal hugs...

51. hug and walk at the same time

52. Real Silly hug: squeeze and both make animal sounds

'You grow up the day you have your first laugh— at yourself.'

-Ethel Barrymore

53. the slow, here I come hug

54. put a stick between you,
try to start a fire

55. the come-prepared hug

'We grow shells to protect ourselves.
Too often the shells become us.'

—Eli J Schleifer

55. (ALTERNATE) hug and tell someone a secret

56. stare into each other's eyes for one minute, then hug

57. 'who'll blink first?' hug

'love is the act of endless forgiveness, a tender look which becomes a habit'
– peter ustinov

58. star gazing hug

'love is the only game that is not called because of darkness'

59. hug your boss
(use the opportunity for the power of suggestion)
give Ed a raise

'If you know God, you know you're loved'
-Robert Schuller

60. hug and say a prayer together (Hug prayers on next page)

61. hug and do a chorus line kick

Hug Prayer #1

O God, I want to belong;
teach me to accept.
I want to be close;
teach me to reach out.
I want a place where I am welcome;
teach me to open my arms.

— Ted Loder
I want to belong
Guerrillas of Grace

hug Prayer #2

Sometimes my heart turns
cold, O God. Forgive me for my
indifference toward others.
Remind me to warmly embrace
others as your love enfolds me.

Amen

62. hug and say 'you're a very special person'

63. the Tango hug

'There is only one happiness in life, to love and be loved'
– George Sand

64. hug a stuffed animal

65. working up to a full hug-
hug just an arm or a leg...

66. hug with an egg between you (hug gently without dropping or breaking egg)

67. the facing away hug

68. hug and say 'I'm glad I'm here holding you'

69. hug without using arms

70. leaning tower of pisa hug

'Love is not measured by how many times you touch each other but by how many times you reach each other.'

-Cathy Morancy

71. hug with a whoopee cushion between you (or make the sounds of a whoopee cushion)

72. how to hug a real sweaty person →

give your partner a choice...

73. how to make sure you get a hug

74 hug with one arm and pat back

'It's not the days of your life that count, but the life in your days'

-Adlai Stevenson

"Laughter is the sun that drives winter from the human face."

—Victor Hugo

75. tell an amusing or funny true story hug

76. hug by candlelight

77. when you're not sure if a hug is appropriate... hug <u>and</u> shake hands

'My friends, how desperately do we need to be loved and to love'

-chief Dan George

78. hug and say 'I love you'

79. ckecking for deodorant hug

80. let your fingers do the walking hug

81. hug with your pet between you

'The most wasted day is that in which we have not laughed.' -Chamfort

82. ear nibble hug

83. hug with funny hats
-switch hats-take a photo

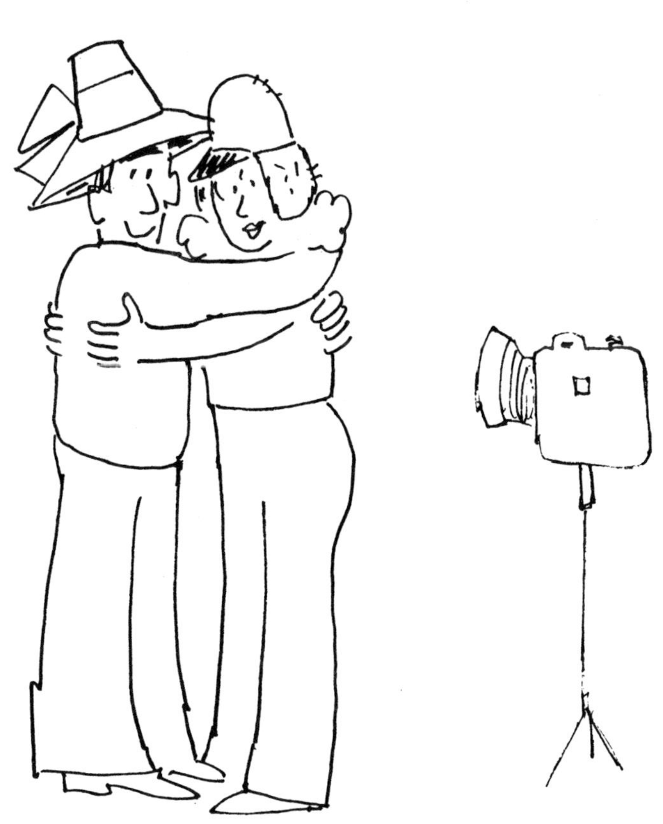

84. Super Soft hug
put a pillow between you

85. statue of liberty hug
(say something patriotic)

'Let there
be spaces
between your
togetherness—
let the winds
of the heavens
dance between
you'

—Kahil Gibran

86. Bear hug (squeeze hard)

87. hug as you bend your knees

88. hug when someone least expects it...

'To love yourself is the beginning of a lifelong romance'
-Oscar Wilde

89. hug yourself
(say out loud one outstanding thing about you)

"The most important things in life are not things."

—Bulletin, First Christian Church, Fairfield, IL

90. the run and hug

"I can't make people like me, but if I wasn't me, I would like me."

—Third grader

91. shrug and hug -
hug and shrug - etc..

92. grab your partner's
garment and hug

93. turn in a circle hug

94. side to side hug

'A good laugh is sunshine in a house.'

-William Makepeace Thackeray

'To get the full value of joy, you must have someone to divide it with'

—Mark Twain

95. hug and tell each other one special thing about one another

96. the flap your arms up and down hug

97. Close your eyes, let God give you a hug (Say something nice about Him)

'Developing a healthy spirituality through reflection and silence contributes to mental health and may even help physical healing'

-Robert J. Wicks

98. twist and shout hug

99. barely touch hug

100. hug and tap your toes to music

'Great joys, like griefs, are silent' -Shackeley Marmion

101. Say and do nothing hug

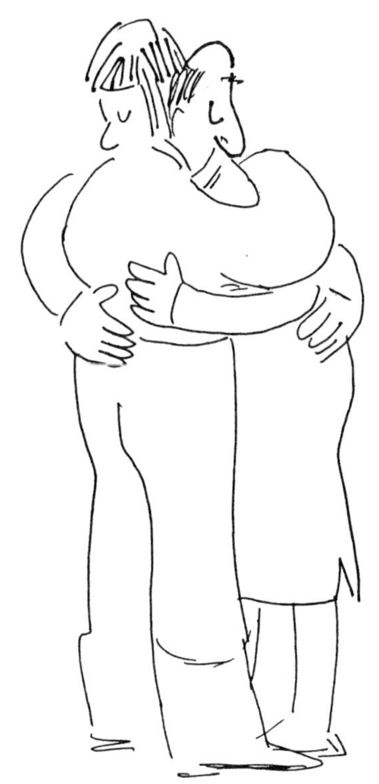